D0096860

# Toucan Nest

# Toucan Nest

Poems of Costa Rica

## Peggy Shumaker

 Red Hen Press | *Pasadena, CA*

*Toucan Nest: Poems of Costa Rica*
Copyright © 2013 by Peggy Shumaker
All Rights Reserved

No part of this book may be used or reproduced in any manner whatsoever without the prior written permission of both the publisher and the copyright owner.

Book design by Mark E. Cull
Book layout by Skyler Schulze

ISBN 978-1-59709-263-0 (tradepaper)
ISBN 978-1-59709-678-2 (clothbound)
Library of Congress Cataloging-in-Publication Data
Shumaker, Peggy, 1952–
Toucan nest : poems of Costa Rica / Peggy Shumaker.—1st ed.
    p. cm.
I. Title.
PS3569.H778T68 2013
811'.54—dc23

                    2012023529

The Los Angeles County Arts Commission, the Los Angeles Department of Cultural Affairs, the City of Pasadena Cultural Affairs Division, Sony Pictures Entertainment, and the Dwight Stuart Youth Fund partially support Red Hen Press. This publication was supported in part by an award from the National Endowment for the Arts.

First Edition
Published by Red Hen Press
www.redhen.org

## Acknowledgments

Grateful thanks to the editors and publishers who first welcomed this work:

*Alaska Quarterly Review*, "Genesis, Quetzal," "Strangler Fig," "Tent Revival"; *Ascent*, "Calls of Birds We Cannot See"; *Blackbird*, "El Laberinto," "Pájaro Sagrado," "Ramón's Eyes"; *Clover, A Literary Rag*, "Ancestor," "How the Motmot Got That Tail"; *The Fiddlehead*, "Mottled Owls, *Parque José Martí*," "Rising Before Sun," "Sloth"; *The Gettysburg Review*, "Flamenco Macaws," "Toucan Nest"; *Hobble Creek Review*, "Blue-Gray Tanager, Here, Gone," "Long Flight, Shadowy Taxi, Garden," "Slaty Flowerpiercer"; *The Los Angeles Review*, "Passion Flower"; *Permafrost*, "In Praise of What Does Not Belong to Us," "In the Shadow of the Guanacaste Tree," "Ride Into Town"; *Prairie Schooner*, "Canopy Walk," "Getting Away," "Losing the Pink Bananas," "Painted Cart with No Oxen," "Slick Trail," "Tucked Deep Among Tangled Roots"; *A River and Sound Review,* "Blue Morpho"; *Superstition Review,* "Lagoon Near La Selva," "Leaf Cutter Ants," "Rain at Trogon Lodge"; and *Verse Wisconsin*, "Gallo Pinto" (online), "Murciélagos," "Spirit of the Bat."

*Fire on Her Tongue: An eBook Anthology of Contemporary Women's Poetry*, ed. Kelli Russell Agodon and Annette Spaulding-Convy (Two Sylvias Press, 2011), "Anhinga Drying Her Wings," "Basilisk Lizard," "Venom."

To Colleen Rooney, naturalist, and Eloise Klein Healy, poet guide, thank you.

With thanks to my hiking, birding, and writing companions in Costa Rica: Nan Cano, Karen Kuester, Regina Lark, Mary Lintula, Rebecca Morse, Maureen O'Connell, Sue Pope, Ronni Sanlo, Georjean Seeliger, Jim Thiele, and Joe Usibelli.

Thank you to our skilled guides, Ramón Valdez and Juan Carlos Rodriguez.

Grateful thanks and admiration to Kate Gale and Mark Cull, and to the staff, interns, and volunteers at Red Hen Press.

PROPERTY OF
LIBRARY OF THE CHATHAMS
CHATHAM NJ

*For Joe, siempre*

# Contents

# Toucan Nest

# Long Flight, Shadowy Taxi, Garden

*—Heredia, Costa Rica*

Birdcalls

deepen

twilight sky

full of want me,

want me. Full-

throated touch.

Moon's veil lifts

the near edge of dusk

lusters a whole world

we don't know.

## In the Shadow of the Guanacaste Tree

"Nearly extinguished,"
    the sign says.

*En peligro*, coffee frogs
    wait till sunset

to sing. From among
    furled hyacinths'

buoyant bulbs
    tentative

    questions rise:
    You think? You think?

                ∽

New hatch—
    blue sparks—

synapse surface
    skitters.

～

We brave
   unstable stones,

bend closer.
   They say

the frogs' rare eyes
   glow golden.

We never see
   a single one.

Not for our eyes
   do those throats

open. We know.
   We know. We know.

# RIDE INTO TOWN

*—San José, Costa Rica*

Downshifting wah-
unce, twi-
ice, little
red taxi barely
pulls the steep
hill, hair-
pins, groans
up and over

along gullies
where kids pick
through the dump,
drag home
long sacks bulged
with whatever they might
use, sell, trade, burn
in squatter shacktowns.

Have the automatic doors
of El Museo del Oro
whooshed open for them?
Have they seen
what their ancestors
plucked from bare dirt,
melted, molded, polished,
buried with their dead?

Shimmery amulets
their legacy—thin
children, shoes
mismatched.
What shamans
heal them?
What rituals
blunt hunger?

## LOSING THE PINK BANANAS

No longer than my fingers,
thicker though, they glowed
rosy, a many-handed begging bowl
held up to the sky.

Huge flower stalk
rose straight up, purple
minaret. So delicate,
so strange, this life.

I wanted to show
my beloved. But
when we retraced
half-remembered steps,

we could not find them.
I asked a man who every day
tends this earth, his life
planting, feeding, cutting back,

and he led us,
laughing, gestured
toward graceful bells
of pink-white ginger,

toward bromeliads,
tiny bird mouths
open inside, toward
crab claws of heliconia,

all the while warning us
we'd need beaks to sample
pink bananas—don't
swallow what's invisible.

## Blue-Gray Tanager, Here, Gone

Pájaro I've pictured
floats, toes open

toward
her perch—

wings backlit
gold-white

ripe color
forty years gone—

my mother,
her hair.

Our dead
appear

vanish.
So much

we can't know.
So we spend

our lives
asking.

*Kind. Joyful and kind,*
he remembers, distant

cousin who knew
her young, poised

for flight
into a sky

cool as the blue
aroma of gardenia

not yet crushed.
Elfin, light—clean brook—

in her path
each root, rock, rough

edge freshens.
Her hair,

white-blonde
halo, fine

as dandelion
fluff. Wave

gathering foam
about to crest.

He knew her.
Remembers

my mother
graceful

before
four kids

before she turned
twenty-four.

## El Laberinto

Bet in the wet it's scary,
circles of hedge above our heads.

Dry season, April, we can see
five or six rows through

so no worries. At the center
a high gazebo, with Escher

mazes morphing. We scan
the whole garden

and beyond. Then backtrack,
perverse, seek out

the dead ends.
A nesting

clay-colored thrush
regards us, beak

trailing untrimmed
a waist-length

beard of moss.
When his mouth's

not full,
he sings the rain.

## Pájaro Sagrado

*—Trogon Lodge, Talamanca Mountains*

Okay, see that
    tall white
        distinctive tree?

Left of that
    tangled
        clump?

Left of that
    straighter
        trunk?

Trace it
    almost
        to the top,

where three
    big branches
        bear left.

Follow the lowest,
    veer off
        on that little switch

and there,
    backlit,
        blink

double quick
    / hold
        breath / sharpen

focus . . . There roosts,
    resplendent
        as promised,

el quetzal.
    Back to us,
        he trails

his tail of light,
    trail we might
        trace

toward quiet.
    Flash of red
        beneath his wing—

he preens,
    whole being
        haloed.

A few steps
    higher, our eyes
        take in

true colors—
    blue green
        of clear sea

over thriving reefs.
    Perhaps he swallowed
        the tiny avocado

he prefers. Maybe
    that's why
        he's so still.

Perhaps, like us,
    he has nowhere
        better to be.

## Genesis, Quetzal

Swallow at dawn one
tiny avocado. Hold so still
the world begins.

Love cry
of the jaguar dyes
crimson

your deepest belly
down. Each glance a
hummingbird, preening,

the narrow trail
of her open bill.
Copper-green wing,

amethyst geode
throat. Blink once
and stars take flight—

sing like trogons, motmots,
yellow-thighed finches, sooty
robins, nightingale thrushes,

acorn carpinteros
tucked into carved-out holes,
wrens and siskins

seen or hidden.
Cataratas, water-
falls of song. Your chest,

vest of drip tips,
highland forest awake
after rain. Breeze-

ruffled streams,
your tails
run to the Pacific,

waves hungry
to mingle
with reef and sand,

velvet green crest,
teal of tide pool.
When you push off,

flowerpiercers and
flycatchers fall
from your feathers.

When you push off,
earth gasps and sighs.
Your wings stir

root aromas tangled
underfoot. When you push off,
cloud and sky

reshape around you.
When you push off,
a new world spins.

## Slaty Flowerpiercer


Nectar drinker, nectar thief,
dusky robber with too-short beak,

from darting sabers you keep
fair distance, sneak

into and through
fuchsias claimed

by fierce competitors.
Hidden by petals,

hidden
by leaves,

you stab a hole
in each corolla,

then lap up sweetness
with your brush-tipped tongue.

Hidden low among
exploded globes

you try not to tzeep,
try not to sing,

leave each flower
weeping nectar.

Nearly snub-nosed
as you,

a volcano
hummingbird

watches it all,
zips in to sip

from wounds
you've left.

To the fuchsia you two
offer no favors.

Pollens you don't
bother to gather,

don't pass along.
Fresh seeds

you don't swallow
then give flight.

Instead you arrive
expecting

to be fed,
adolescents

pretty sure this world's
yours to devour.

# Rain at Trogon Lodge

*—Talamanca Mountain Highlands*

Pura vida come purer,
bromeliads replenish
tiny lakes entrusted to their
calderas. Calla lilies
stiffen, sway.

Darting hummers, purple-
throated, green-winged,
whir feeder to fuchsia,
rafter to fig.
Drenched, the world

shimmers—pearls
suspend
along dark
soffits. Elastic
drops

shape-shift—
puddle, fishpond,
cloud breath.
Iguana's drink, our
moist souls' scrim.

## RAMÓN'S EYES

He must be part iguana, one eye
fast on gravel curves, one eye
scanning the canopy.

Even when he points,
patiently
explains,

half the time, we're blind.
Driving the bus, he guides us
toward sight.

He's sharp as razor wire
no matter where we are—
city, cloud forest, coast.

In the rainforest,
Ramón
speaks quetzal,

whistles tanager, thrush,
hummingbird, finch,
sooty robin, wren.

When he calls,
they come closer,
curious.

He's silent, though,
reverent
when the giant tinamu

with no warning
meanders
across our path.

Cousin to the vireo, Ramón,
ruby eyes flaming, builds a
cup nest in the canopy.

He catches in bare hands
a tiny flash of green—
speckled *ranita*,

poison dart frog,
set out so we can see.
Our leader says,

*See what Ramón*
*just did?*
*Don't do that.*

~

Dust so thick, we lose
the truck in front,
the one behind.

An oxcart lunges
up onto roadtop,
overloaded, red tangles

of just-harvested
palm nuts, black knobs
pressed for oil.

Along the coast,
Ramón swerves to the verge,
sets the brake.

In one tree,
two, three,
six macaws, raucous,

twenty now,
scarlet,
on the wing.

～

Ramón directs us
to the roadside stand
where on the last day

he picks up queso,
mango, heart-shaped
milk candies. Home.

If you ever fly north,
Ramón, nuestro casa
es su casa.

Ramón's eyes fill—
*Y mi casa es suyos . . .*
is small, my house,

but yours.
Ramón, whose daughter chose
for her *quinceañera*

six friends from school,
a cake her mamá baked,
and her family.

Ramón glances cloudward
for the rains, season
when he rests

in his own nest
after months on the road
barely blinking.


*for Ramón Valdez, with thanks*

## Mottled Owls, *Parque José Martí*

Asleep, thanks, this being daylight,
burrowing deep in one another,

chest feathers better
than any pillow.

Below you, two men
set out checkers,

bottle caps from two brands,
turned up as kings.

The one who hasn't had a stroke
allows his friend to take his time.

The one who has
wins half the time.

Schoolchildren can't believe
our stories of rivers of ice.

They grin, try to figure out
the lie. Then run,

because they can, run
everywhere, waving

behind them as our bus
chugs away,

our heads
swiveling owls.

# Sloth

Thirty feet up, not so
slow as we thought, honey-
blonde three-toed

perezosa
spans the great Y
between branches. Arced

claws unfold, cutlery
close at hand.
She hangs wide

open, a great gold X
crossing paths with
the bloodied man

thorn-torn in cathedrals.
Her tongue dangles
moist leaves.

Foot over hand, her
gradual shifts
sculpt

time.
She's at home
in dense fur.

We groundlings
suffer dripping
coats of salt.

Why should
her pace
suggest sin?

Her quizzical
face, placid
as faith

that one day
visions might catch up
to endless questions.

## Flamenco Macaws

Two scarlet
macaws flirt, hang up-

side down,
dinky limb spring-

loaded—foot-
treadle Singers

stitching backless
costumes. Flamenco

*gritos*, shout
*alegrias*, tassled

shawls swirl. Palmas
offbeat synch-

opate castanets.
Fire-tempered lovers

yell, whole courtyard
awake now. Whirlwind

de colores, forty
wings of ruby flames,

RAACK-RAACK
outlined against sea-salt back-

drop, wild spiral
flight, three turns

till clawed toes clench
scarred branches tight.

## Keeping Loud Ones Quiet

"You love macaws, right?
My great aunt
has a scarlet macaw,
her best friend."

Eloise hesitates,
doesn't say, "I'd like to strangle
your great aunt."
"Here's the deal," she says.

That cherished pet, wings
clipped, neurotic,
pampered with sleigh bells and plastic
globes whirling

has for twenty years
heard no voice
from her flock, seen
no feather except

in mirrors. She's never
flown, though she still
stretches cut wings
through her dreams.

For this confined life
a hundred birds died,
hatchlings poached
from borderline nests

wet forest, dry forest,
park and preserve.
Packed in wheel wells,
in false-bottomed vans,

in car doors and camper
shells, in crates
and cages, drugged
to keep them quiet . . .

In shock, in disguise
as boots or masks,
stuffed into jacket
pockets, wings banded

they flew, baggage
undeclared. They bumped
dusty over gravel
byways. Some arrived

breathing, panicky,
revived in Tokyo, London,
Paris, Newark,
L.A., Oaxaca,

Des Moines.
Lucky, *las lapas*
left to the sky.
Not so the thousands

caged and admired
the hundreds
of thousands
plucked or dumped.

What we love
we hold close.
We bring to our eyes
expensive glass,

draw what's wild into heart
and mind. Celebrate this moment
on the wing, twenty macaws,
scarlet flock squawking.

## Calls of Birds We Cannot See

Sunlight through red veins

of coleus. Your palm

dawns on me.


Corrugated hailstorms—

metal roof, earthquake

of ten-pound iguanas.

Shy thicket bird, ancient

tinamu steps out

among newcomers.

Honor flows both ways.


Three agouti bow

to the rushing stream.

Far cries of howler monkeys

turn our heads.

Towering stand—

giant bamboo

tonks and groans,

arthritic pirate ship

overladen with lost

dreams, bones.


Birds we most desire

se vuelve, se fué.

Tiny black frog

Ramón delicately sets

on a stump—bright green

markings, our innocence.


Snakes, bats, a lost

fanny pack, zipping

heights, steep downhill

hike, the dead sure

bite of all we fear.

Prim British laydee

with perfect posture,

wizened pair of marimba

players, six mallets

bouncing out "El Rancho

Grande." The guitarist's

wink. A widow,

this dancer. Her vow

never to sit out

another *baile*.

## TOUCAN NEST

Cautious as a stalked ex,
chestnut mandibled toucan

profiled in a far triangle
makes sure no one's tailing her . . .

then shoves off. Quick
flight, te dé, te dé,

toward lofty hollows.
The tree swallows

her great curved face, yellow
bib, red belly, dainty

blue legs. Inside the tree
nest shrieks of hunger.

Within the living
trunk, true shelter

of decay. She cracks
her bill to spill

half-digested
fruits and lizards

down yawning
gullets,

cramming four
unfeathered young.

It's her secret
tucked tree deep

how she turns in there,
emerges

tip first,
half of her

that gleaming bill
serrated yellow

spliced brown,
dangling shreds

she shows her throat
to swallow.

## LLUVIA

Thunder slides
   down the zip line.

Sky water
   quickens

murky streams
   where, motionless,

striped tiger heron
   hunts.


—*Río Savegre*

## At Villa Lapas

She likes being called señorita,
stout woman grilling

fresh talápia to go
with green plantain ceviche.

Gracias, I nod.
Con gusto, she smiles—

*with pleasure*—
much more gracious

than No problem,
You got it, De nada,

No sweat.
Behind her grill

she glistens.
Con gusto.

## Leaf Cutter Ants

Scouts lay out
scent trails
to meal-ticket trees.

Foragers clear paths
trudging
nest to source,

source to nest,
lugging green sails,
forest regatta,

tiny stowaway
high in each crow's nest
keeping an eye out,

in for the long haul,
whole colony's
hitchhiking conscience.

Far down
in chambers, minims
farm fungi, nourish

hard workers,
the burgeoning
brood. Beneath

our feet, strength
in numbers
enormous enough

to undermine church
and state,
homes, gravestones,

any monument
our crew of latecomers
pictures as permanent.

# How the Motmot Got That Tail

When Sibo asked
every creature to help
make the world,

the motmot
hid
in a hole.

All the other animals,
all the other birds,
did their share.

A tattler saw
the motmot's tail,
plucked out one feather

then another. All the birds
chipped in, plucked.
Tired out just before they finished.

When the world was complete,
Sibo gave the birds a rest.
Motmot showed up, bragged

I did more than
all of you put together!
But his tail

testified.
He could not hide
his lazy behind.

## VENOM

The gardener
bashes in

the gorgeous
triangular head

of the fer-de-lance,
most venomous

víbora he knows.
Ay!  One bite

and you're dead.
His forked stick

lifts looped,
lank snake,

draped away
from his legs.

I ask to look—
slithers to earth

spoiled coil
turned clay.

*Hermosa*, I sigh.
Mosaic

scales, cream,
black, brown.

He nods.
*Hermosa y*

*peligrosa. Muy*
*peligrosa.*

Our guide
conjures prayers,

apologies.
The forked stick

slings pure danger
behind the shed.

## Basilisk Lizard

Lusty jitterbug
amplified by
corrugated rust

scares the bejesus
out of us. Before
roof flakes

settle, freckle
rust-earth
tiles, you skitter

toward water. Your toes
hinge over, longer
than your feet.

Little king, named
for a made-up
mess, part rooster,

part dragon, part
snake, you're very much awake
cooling your tail in the pool,

lifting, alert,
to every footfall,
wingbeat, breath.

With a single glance,
the story goes,
the basilisk

could stop
a heart. One step
too close

and you're
panic incarnate—
Jesus Christ

Lizard zipping
zigzag on hind legs,
kicking up

trails of rain,
salvation's sip sip
sip into mist.


*for Bill Kloefkorn*

## Canopy Walk

Bridges give,
swing underfoot, hold
us suspended

eighty feet up
among towering
rainforest treetops.

Twelve at once
cross—steps
shudder—

bridge ripples
each boot,
shifts

solid assumptions,
our weight no longer
where we planted.

Over the edge,
strangler figs
tangle, never-

ending lawsuits
starving out
root and branch

of one that lifted
toward light
tiny-rooted

epiphyte
that took over
this host's life.

Now, reaching down,
the bountiful fig
sinks in, offers

shelter, food,
its questionable
example

to all creatures
from fern-glade
forest floor

through each branching
story
up

into canopy,
green arc of
breath above us.

GETTING AWAY

We sidewind inside clouds
along ridgelines dividing
waters that shed east
from waters that shed west—

el páramo, which I know
only from Pedro, the Páramo
from Comala, hometown so hot
dead folks arriving in Hell

go back to get their blankets.
In the Talamancas, rufous-
naped sparrows shove mashed-up
worms beak to beak.

We glide down, down, toward
the Tárcoles River, where
twenty crocs per kilometer
make their ancient living

except here, at the bridge,
where dozens of huge ones
snap and shove, chomp down
junk that people throw.

Around the bend, spoonbills,
rosy and plump, strain
rivermuck. By treadless tires
wood storks hunker, shoulders hunched.

Quick plovers and stilts
pace cuneiform messages.
Green herons call, call
downriver, then follow

their voices. Lone
royal egret paces very near
two half-submerged
relics plastered in mud.

They're sharp toothed, zap
fast, fuerte. But she
can lift
up out of silt and soar.

## Painted Cart with No Oxen

Legend has it that in ancestral
forest under a waning moon
church carpenters cut
bitter cedar for a new altar,

bitter cedar for new saints.
They stacked chopped logs
outside their workshop,
curled into their hammocks.

That fingernail of light
let the stars shine brighter.
Two former altar boys
crept up, rolled the logs

into the river. They rode them
the long way home.
When the wood dried,
they built a shelter

for their mother, a table,
a bench, and then
crafted an oxcart sturdier
than anyone had ever seen.

On it their sister painted
curls, feathers,
their mother's favorite flowers,
triangles in all colors,

silk threads and broad swaths,
a circle of pompiniado,
colors of bird, stone,
volcano, ocean.

Priests warned from the pulpit
that coffee plants
would bear no cherries,
that fish would slip out

of mended nets,
that milk cows would
go dry, and chickens
stop laying—all this

and roasting in Hell
would befall
whoever had stolen
the sacred wood.

But the former altar boys
knew from older stories
that the roots of the
bitter cedar speak

through their branches
to the stars. And the stars,
brighter tonight, heard
their prayers, their thanks

for shelter, for a table,
for a cart of many colors
that they hauled themselves
bringing in their mother's harvest,

their crippled neighbor's
harvest, more coffee
than ever, hauled without help
to a town downstream.

San José,
a carpenter too, watched
all this from on high.
He liked the spirit

of these brothers in wood.
He sent them on a detour
on the way home, past
a farm where twin oxen

had just been born. They traded
the promise of hauling
for the newborns, loaded them
onto fresh leaves in the cajón,

pulled with their own muscles
in the last light of the stars,
pulled twin oxen in the painted cart
back to their fields, back home.

## Rising Before Sun

Wild, the Montezuma
Oropéndola's bobble-note shout-
shout while it bows, bows,

bows so low
Oropéndola nearly topples, up-
ended tail fan

amarillo
bright caution.
Shout-shout Oropéndola

over chachalacas walking
bare branches, tending
tangentially toward

freckled bananas.
Oropéndola's great orange
bill pierces a peel.

When she opens
her mouth, day-
light spreads.

## SLICK TRAIL

Starless night's
steady downpour

we savor,
much-scarred

familiars
waking

with love touch,
freshened,

rising
lipmoist,

voyagers
via rainforest

aromas, trails
cascading

seven pools
below us,

watershiver
hummingbirds

snowcap, female
scooping, shaking,

snowcap, male
quietly bathing,

third pool
theirs alone.

Each pond
reserved,

one mirror
per species.

## Tent Revival

If after
afternoon rains
you hang
under a blue tarp
this worn bedsheet,

then position
behind it a lamp
and before it a bench,
all manner of visitors
will descend.

Most wish you no harm.
Invertebrates smaller
than the nail
on an infant's little finger
tremble, backlit

beside luna moths
wide as masks
feathered for carnival.
Mosaic in motion,
triangles of tent-wings.

Tatted, bobbin spun,
hardanger, crewel work—
the delicacy and strength
of lace. Sepia ink
on hand-laid paper,

openwork cut
with manicure scissors.
One magnificent
jeweled fellow—
cloisonné patterns

red-brown and tan—
twirls antennae
twice his length,
draws the world
to him, to him, to him.

Dripping still,
water flows over us,
carves fresh paths
down the mountain,
and underground.

Strangers here,
we draw this world
to us, to us, to us,
world we've just begun
to sense, to take in.

## In Praise of What
## Does Not Belong to Us

Let's not mourn
quick glimpses
of crest, of wing,
not waste one moment

cursing slow
reflexes, dim
eyes, fumbled
focus.

Listen.

Mystery fruits
split last night
draw beetles,
tanagers, motmots,

draw wrens to feast
on semillas, seeds.
Everywhere birds go
drop chances

for new caimitos.
Aves call, deep
in leaves
all around us.

We seldom see
more than swoop,
flash,
gone.

Listen . . .

Breathe deep
green lemon blossoms
of song sung in tongues
juicy as mangoes.

## Dantica / Tapir

In cloud forest, this—
corrugated metal roof covering an
exquisite glass-walled gallery
run by a skinny man from Amsterdam
and a green-eyed beauty from Colombia.
In ultra-modern curves of Danish
white ware they offer us
fine Costa Rican coffees.
Hardwood crackles in metal,
upended funnel fireplace six inches
from floor-to-ceiling
glass, walls affording us
the grand expanse—montañas,
valleys, hillsides, sky.

We settle in. He starts
a video—irritating
voiceover, badly
translated script, but we're
hooked anyway. Somewhere
deeper in jungle than we are,
women weave on waist-looms
nubbly textiles. One whole town
pulls the devil's face
from wood. Our host hands around
a woven vase—months it takes
to harvest, dry, split, dye,
dry again, split thin strips, then
weave vessels so tight they carry water.

Behind us
KA-THWACK!
sickening thud
as if skulls smacked
a windshield—
highways of cracks
remap the wall of glass.
Nervous, broken
shards of laughter.

The skinny owner,
an optimist,
assures us the timing
couldn't be better. Already
the glazier's coming
in a couple of days,
hauling all the way
from San José
two panes now.

We gather grass bracelets,
masks no more devilish
than our secrets,
tiny gold frogs.
We stop resisting
the orange and black
geometry of one
vessel of water, vessel
of grace, vessel of fire.

## Burnt Fields

Panicked iguanas hustle,
rough-winged swallows
sky-skitter,
víboras in furrows

slither when farmers
on purpose
to rid cane of razors
set fire to ripe fields.

Choking clouds of flamed
sugar billow,
balloon. Three soot-streaked men
machete-whack stalks,

sweat dripping
as if they're melting.
Sharp edges—
skin's cut

right through wet shirts.
Crosshatched scars
one shade lighter
track hard muscles.

Fangs men's sharp eyes
watch for
wait, coils
of poison. Costly

sweetness, smudged.
Rice and beans
this sugar buys,
schoolbooks, *zapatos.*

Tongue touch
of pleasure—
in *café con leche,*
in shots of guaro

at Sabado's *baile.*
Haystack high
scorched cut cane
stragglers overflow

wood slat and wire wagons,
grimy old tractor straining
uphill to the crusher, up to the mill,
man-high grass hacked to stubble.

## Cloud Forest Trail

Whirring frenzy—chitter
as if they mean to probe
my ears for nectar—
motley humming flock
whips up misty air.
Band-tailed barbthroat,
rufous-tailed, long-billed
hermit, wood nymph,

green-breasted, violet-crowned,
sabrewing, fierce purple-green
Jacobin. Slick flick of humming-
birds' tongues. Guainambí.
Emerald, ruby, star-
throat. Iridescent,
impulse-quick—
desire given wing.

## Strangler Fig

Cousins, then,
the myriad orchids
of the mist forest
and this towering
strangler fig.

Both start
tenuous life
as stowaways
tossed aside
by wind or wing

dropped
without anyone's
noticing
high above
the forest floor.

Air plants,
epiphytes, bromeliads
plastered so heavy
some branches
crack, tumble.

But the fig's patient.
It settles in,
sucks what it can
from leaf rot, from
breaks in bark,

drinks deep
from fine mist.
Then into air
fig tentacles
unfurl, aiming

toward the host's
small patch of soil.
Fig leaves above
cover all else.
Not out of modesty.

Each fig takes its own
special wasp
to carry on,
wasp that swaps
pollen for protection.

Nearly gone,
the host lingers
within the fig
like the memory
of a difficult parent

who never knew
what she was taking on
when she got you,
mother who resented
being tied down,

mother whose face
you can't quite
picture, mother
who changed so much
those last years

you barely knew her,
broken mother
asthmatic, wheezy,
who gave her all
so you might live.

## Lagoon Near La Selva

Through binocs, we bring close
slash eye of the caiman, still

spalted log,
nostril skimming . . .

splash-grab and toothchomp,
headshake and swallow

murkclouds at pond edge
settle to dank

shoal. Rusty sheen
burnishes the wood rail's wing.

Bare-throated tiger heron
tilts on his snag.

Ringed kingfisher rattles,
fresh from her riverbank,

mud-walled tunnel where
parents trade off tending

from this season's clutch
one chick left.

## Ancestor

There, claws sunk in a river snag,
hangs a wrinkly skinned

iguana as long as I am tall.
I can't explain his goiter, nor

the prickles beneath his chin.
Along his back vestigial spines

droop like a bad comb-over.
One eye he keeps on us

while we steal closer.
Why hang there in the heat,

instead of bellying up
to the mudbank?

Maybe to him, one
who must take in

whatever warmth
he's going to have,

this choking sauna's
as close to nirvana

as this incarnation's
going to get.

## Howler Monkeys

The parents, like most parents, yell.
A lot. But little ones hang
by the tips of their tails,

sail off into space, misjudge
the next branch,
crash through

limbs and leaves,
catch
themselves,

carry on
as if they've got a lifetime
maybe more.

Mangoes ripe
*right now*
drip down their elbows.

Tomorrow
has yet
to occur to them.


—*Río Sarapiquí*

# ANHINGA DRYING HER WINGS

Purely practical, we know,
her need to hold herself open

to let what sun she can catch
ease the river from her wings.

And yet. And yet.

## Mangrove Swamp

Salted, the estuary,
then refreshed.

Buttresses breathe
where mangroves

tangle,
the manglar's

intricate city
of roots

scooping silt
so reefs

don't smother.
Tides come,

tides go,
moon-pulled.

Sweating salt
from top leaves,

red mangroves
count on rains.

Prop roots
suck up oxygen.

One claw huge, one small,
the fiddler

crab-walks
the root maze

among algae,
corals, sponges.

In his path
fretful tracework

of elegant
writing,

a language
we knew once

when our roots
sank deep

when our roots
breathed for us

when our roots
spanned yesterday

& tomorrow,
roots for every

being living,
bound for life.

## Tucked Deep among Tangled Roots

In mangrove swamp,
one tree flowers.

One tree opens
in white blossom.

And one bird,
one tiny bird

whirring so fast
we nearly miss

her green blur,
one bird

treats this flower
as if her life

depends upon it.


*(Buttressed tea mangrove flower,*
*mangrove hummingbird)*

## Mariposas

Meshed garden of wings
Chrysalis earrings

Red-black scales
Too moist yet to fly

Handspan of tan camo
Heart slash of Blue Morpho

Cocoons of one life
So few days, egg to end

## BLUE MORPHO

At rest, false eyes
spot us,

your legs tasting
half-fermented mango,

rippling proboscis
sipping rank juice.

One startled slash—
bright shimmer—

ocean sixty feet down,
earth seen from space,

longing held
too long

song of one long gone,
that blue.

Not what you absorb, but
what you can't take in—

that's what we see
of your beauty.

## Murciélagos

Near La Selva,
orange bats skim low

to gaff with their hook-feet
live fish they like to eat.

With very long legs
and enormous feet

their pups
wait in sea caves

four months
before new wings

can hold them up,
four months

hanging around
upside down,

nothin' to do.
*Eat it all, bones,*

*head, tail,*
*fins,* their parents

insist. They know

that barking
with a full mouth

won't echo,
won't reveal

ripples barely
below the surface,

flash of scales
whipping fins

skittery school
of the colony's

next meal.
At night

we read
promises

in field guides,
promises

in dreams. You
whir below patios,

skim over waves.
Cousins with wings—

déjà vu, don't
we know you?


*(Murciélagos Pescadores, fishing bulldog bats)*

ECHOES

Because they find their way in starlight.
Because after dark they whiz through moist air.
Because they fold and unfold, warm themselves
    with fabric they use to fly.
Because even in daylight we can't be sure
    they're asleep.
Because they come from a long line of tricksters.
Because if they can't find mango, can't find guava,
    they open blossoms.
Because pollens adorn them, because pollens
    alight where they rest.
Because seeds they digest are ready.
Because their guano nourishes.
Because very few spread rabies.
Because fear spreads faster than disease.
Because fear is married to hatred, so many die.
Because those who die may be harmless, may be helpful.
Because the world in fear does not distinguish.

## Spirit of the Bat

Hair rush, low swoop—
so those of us

stuck here on earth
know—you must be gods.

Or friends of gods,
granted chances

to push off into sky,
granted chances

to hear so well
your own voice bounced

back to you
maps the night.

Each hinge
in your wing's

an act of creation.
Each insect

you snick out of air
a witness.

You transform
obstacles

into sounds,
then dodge them.

## Gallo Pinto

Fuel for the man
with an earache, waiting,
fuel for the schoolgirl,
her period late,

fuel for the too-tall
*farmacéutica*—
beanstalk
*gallo pinto.*

Breakfast, *almuerzo*,
dinner, snack—
cumin, cilantro,
black beans, rice.

Fuel for crazed
drivers whipping
blind around
curves, *gallo*

*pinto.* Fuel for
cart drivers
calming
yoked oxen.

Fuel for surveyors
taking the long view,
fuel in black-veiled
acres of fronds.

Fuel for waiters'
aching arches,
fuel for drummers,
teachers, potters.

For house painters
speckled
*azul, limón,*
vivid *gallo pinto.*

For blacksmiths
twisting *tico*
window iron,
well-wrought

*gallo pinto.*
Fuel for unwinders
of razor wire,
homeowners

imprisoned.
For gun-toting
thieves, chopped
*gallo pinto.*

For armed guards
outside *Rosti-Pollo*, fuel.
Fuel for drug runners
speeding through.

Half rations
for wrecked plywood
Nicaraguans, ramshackle
rusty *gallo pinto*.

Fuel for the sorrowful
mourners straggled
behind that sealed casket.
Loved one's last meal, *gallo pinto*.

Fuel for the woman
sweating in labor,
woman about to give birth
to the world. *Gallo pinto*.

## PASSION FLOWER

Low over this narrow strand
of land between great oceans,
one named for peace,

one named for Atlas,
who lifts the sky
above the waters,

we're airborne—edging
home, returning changed
to places we know better

than to take for granted.
Over the sea
named for Caribs

nearly wiped out
by disease,
we sip iced water.

Just hours ago
we gazed into the face
of passion

flowering this morning—
pura vida
most alive

on tenuous edges
between hungry seas.
Witness this moment

set off
by our brief passage.
What came before,

what comes after,
the verge ourselves
alive, opening.

BIOGRAPHICAL NOTE


Peggy Shumaker served as Alaska State Writer Laureate from 2010–2012. Her previous books of poems include *Underground Rivers*, *Blaze* (with paintings by Kesler E. Woodward), and *Gnawed Bones*. Her lyrical memoir is *Just Breathe Normally*. *Toucan Nest* grew from an eco-arts writing workshop in Costa Rica. Professor emerita from University of Alaska Fairbanks, Shumaker teaches in the Rainier Writing Workshop. She is founding editor of Boreal Books, publisher of literature and fine art from Alaska. She edits the Alaska Literary Series at University of Alaska Press.

Please visit her website at www.peggyshumaker.com.